Thinking about the Seasons

Winter

Clare Collinson

SEA-TO-SEA
Mankato Collingwood London

This edition first published in 2011 by
Sea-to-Sea Publications
Distributed by Black Rabbit Books
P.O. Box 3263, Mankato, Minnesota 56002

Copyright © Sea-to-Sea Publications 2011

Printed in China, Dongguan

Library of Congress Cataloging-in-Publication Data

Collinson, Clare.
  Winter / Clare Collinson.
     p. cm. -- (Thinking about the seasons)
  Includes index.
  ISBN 978-1-59771-262-0 (library bound)
 1. Winter--Juvenile literature. I. Title.
  QB637.8.C65 2011
  508.2--dc22

                                   2009052822

9 8 7 6 5 4 3 2

Published by arrangement with the Watts Publishing Group Ltd, London.

Planning and production by Discovery Books Limited
Managing editor: Laura Durman
Editor: Clare Collinson
Picture researcher: Rachel Tisdale
Designer: Ian Winton

Photographs: Corbis: p. 7 (Alexander Burkatovski); FLPA: p. 19 (John Hawkins); Getty Images: p. 6 (David Ellis), p. 8 (Mitchell Frank), p. 10 (Image Source), p. 12 (Digital Vision), p. 17 (Koki Iino), p. 21 (Bob Elsdale), p. 23 (Archibald Thorburn), p. 28 (JGI), p. 29 (Billy Hustace), p. 31 (Siman Winnall); istockphoto.com: p. 4 (digitalskillet), p. 9 (Jean Frooms), p. 11 (Chepko Danil), p. 13 (Stuart Hannagan), p. 16 (Jani Bryson), p. 18 (Frank Leung), p. 24 (wuqa), p. 26 (pixartdesign), p. 27 (Doug Berry), p. 30 (xyno6); Shutterstock Images: title page (AGphotographer), p. 5 (Dan Briski), p. 15 (Hallgerd), p. 20 (Dave McAleavy), p. 22 (Glen Gaffney).

Cover photos: main: Getty Images (Ariel Skelley); top corner: Shutterstock Images (Pchemyan Georgiy).

Page 7 *The Boulevard Montmartre, Paris* (1897), Camille Pissarro
Page 14 *Winter Landscape with Skaters and a Bird Trap* (1565), Pieter Brueghel the Younger
Page 23 *Hare* (1920–21), Archibald Thorburn

"The Central Heating" by John Foster (1991) from *Four o'Clock Friday* (Oxford University Press) is included by permission of the author. The publishers regret that they have been unable to trace the copyright holder of the poem "The Snowman" (p. 25). Every attempt has been made to clear copyright. Should there be any inadvertent omission please apply to the Publishers for rectification.

March 2010
RD/6000006414/002

Contents

When I think of winter,
I think of cold weather.
I spend more time inside
in winter, but if I dress really
warm, it can be fun to play outside!

What makes you think of winter?

Winter is one of the four seasons of the year—spring, summer, fall, and winter. The sun rises late in winter, and it sets early, so winter days are short.

How do you think birds and other animals survive the cold winter months?

Even when the sun is shining in winter,
the air can feel very cold.
On winter mornings,
the ground may be
covered with frost.

Have you noticed
the feel of cold,
crisp air on frosty
winter mornings?

This painting makes me think of gray winter afternoons, when the air feels damp and the sky is cloudy. It gets dark early in winter and streetlights help people see where they are going.

When it is very cold, sleet or snow falls instead of rain. Heavy snow and icy roads make traveling difficult.

In winter, people work hard to keep the roads safe. In icy weather, I often see trucks spreading salt on the roads or snowplows clearing snow.

How do you think spreading salt makes the roads safer?

In winter, I spend lots of time inside, where it's warm. I like it when my friends come to my house and we play boardgames and do puzzles.

What games do you like to play inside in winter?

The Central Heating

There's a monster that haunts our house—
It's called the central heating
From the way its stomach rumbles,
Goodness knows what it's been eating!

It wakes us up at nighttime
With its gurglings and its groanings,
Its clattering and its clanging,
Its mutterings and moanings.

Mom says it lives on water,
In answer to my question.
I think that it must gulp it down
To get such indigestion!

John Foster

On winter mornings,
I put on clothes that
will keep me warm.

Why is it a good idea to wear lots of layers in winter?

When I go outside, I wear a coat.
Gloves stop my fingers from getting cold.

On really cold days, I wear
a hat and scarf.

What clothes do
you wear in winter?

This painting makes me think of trees in winter. Many trees lose their leaves during fall and in winter, their branches are bare.

When do leaves begin to grow on the trees again?

Evergreen trees stay green all winter. They have tough, narrow leaves called needles, which can survive cold winter weather.

Have you noticed the fresh, woody smell of pine needles?

I like to eat hot food in winter. I often have oatmeal for breakfast. It helps me keep warm. I like to drink hot chocolate, too.

In winter, I eat lots of vegetables, such as carrots, potatoes, and broccoli. Winter vegetables taste delicious in warming soups and stews.

What foods do you like to eat in winter?

In winter, I often see birds eating berries. There is not much food for birds in winter. There are few insects and, when the ground is hard or frozen, it is difficult for them to find worms and snails to eat.

In winter, I put nuts and seeds outside for hungry birds to eat. I also put water out for birds to drink.

Why is it a good idea to leave water out for birds in winter?

It can be hard for
wild animals to find
enough food in
winter. Some animals migrate. This means
they spend the winter in places where the
weather is warmer and food is easier to find.

Why do you think these swans fly south from Iceland for the winter?

Other animals find different ways to survive the winter. Dormice stay in a deep sleep called hibernation. They wake up again in spring.

Do you know any other animals that hibernate?

Have you noticed that cats and dogs have thicker coats in winter? Some wild animals, such as foxes, also grow thicker fur to help them to stay warm.

Do you know any other animals that have thick fur to keep them warm?

This painting shows a mountain hare. Mountain hares have brown coats in summer, but in winter their fur is white. How do you think this helps them survive?

When there is lots of snow, it's fun to build a snowman. I give my snowman a face and use a bucket for his hat.

What other things do you like doing when it snows?

The Snowman

One day we built a snowman,
We built him out of snow;
You should have seen how fine he was,
All white from top to toe.

We poured some water over him,
To freeze his legs and ears;
And when we went indoors to bed,
We thought he'd last for years.

But, in the night a warmer kind
Of wind began to blow;
And Jack Frost cried and ran away,
And with him went the snow.

When we went out next morning
To bid our friend "good day,"
There wasn't any snowman there...
He'd melted right away!

In winter, I like to play
hockey and go skating.
When it is too cold and wet for outdoor sports,
I play games inside, such as basketball.

In some places, there is snow on the ground all winter. Deep snow is good for skiing and snowboarding.

What games and sports do you play in winter?

When I think of winter, I think of festivals and parties! At Christmas, I send cards to my friends and help decorate the Christmas tree. I love Christmas!

Many people celebrate New Year with music, dancing, and fireworks. The Chinese New Year is an important Chinese festival. In many countries around the world, there are special street parades.

Can you think of any other winter festivals?

As the winter months pass by, I begin to look for signs of spring. Not many flowers bloom in winter. When I see snowdrops, I know that spring is coming soon.

As winter gradually turns to spring, the days become warmer. It stays light for longer, and I can begin to play outside again after school.

What other signs of spring have you noticed at the end of winter?

Index